NFTS AND THEIR HISTORY

EXPLAINING HOW NFT AND BLOCKCHAIN WORK AND THEIR HISTORY

Michelle Rafferty

TABLE OF CONTENT

Introduction

NFT is getting more popular because it is more economical and produces bigger profits, thus, stimulating the interest of the population. This book will teach you all you need to know about NFT and Crypto Art. NFTs are the abbreviation for non-fungible tokens, and an NFT is analogous to the playing card you've already collected as a child in the digital world. Video, artwork, audio, and even book all are possibilities in NFT technology. It's just a virtual document containing ownership information saved on theBlockchain, and that's all there is to it. NFTs are currently thriving invarious fields, and they will have a substantial impact on the creative world shortly.

If you're a writer, you should pay attention to how they should disrupt the industry. A digital commodity that may understand actual goods, including music, artwork, in-game items, and movies—NFTs are becoming morepopular. However, even though they had been around since the early 2000s, NFTs are gradually becoming more popular as a method of making online artwork. Hackers may readily replicate vector illustrations on the web; but, if you utilize NFTs, you'll discover a way of preserving a track record of possession or authenticity that can be used to protect your intellectualproperty. Are you ready to make your first non-fungible token investment? Do you have the necessary funds?

When learning about the intricate realm of NFTs, the NFTs industry, and making more educated decisions in the virtual token business, this bookwill serve you as an excellent beginning point. In today's marketplace, thereis a range of systems available to aid users in getting started with NFT trading. This book is meant to offer you the knowledge and skills necessary to succeed in NFT trading, with the overall objective of securing the financial freedom of its readers. Most people your age isn't exposed to this kind of stuff, so proceed with caution. Please treat nature with respect and understand its value.

The essential thing to do is put it to appropriate use. It's incredibly potent, and if you put in the necessary work and time, it has the potential to revolutionize your life dramatically. Here's what you'll learn about making money as a non-traditional investor and why investing with them is a smart choice!

Chapter 1 - What Are NFTs?

A non-fungible token, likewise termed NFT, is a type of data unit that is both unique and non-transferable, held on a blockchain, a kind of digital ledger. NFTs can be connected with digital items that can be reproduced, such as photographs, movies, and audio. NFTs use a digital ledger to give a certificate of authenticity/evidence of ownership. Still, they do not prohibit exchanging or duplicating the actual digital files stored on the computer. Because NFTs are not interchangeable (fungible), they differ from blockchain-based cryptocurrencies such as Bitcoin in this respect. When it comes to the energy costs and carbon footprint connected with confirming blockchain transactions, as well as their widespread usage in art frauds, NFTs have come under fire. Further concerns question the utility of producing evidence of ownership in a market that is frequently uncontrolled and beyond the legal system.

Reality of NFTs

Non-fungible tokens are cryptographic assets that exist on a blockchain and are distinguished from one another by having unique identifier codes and information. Unlike cryptocurrencies, they cannot be traded or swapped at face value. It is indifferent to fungible tokens, such as cryptocurrencies, which are all identical and may be used as a medium for economic transactions to be carried out. Bitcoin and other cryptocurrencies, like actual money, are fungible, which means that they may be traded or swapped for one another. For example, the value of a single Bitcoin is always the same as the value of another Bitcoin. Similarly, one Ethereum is always equivalent to another unit of Ether. Because of their fungibility, cryptocurrencies are well-suited for use as a safe means of exchange in the digital economy, where they have gained widespread acceptance.

Because each token is exclusive and irreplaceable, NFTs alter the cryptographic paradigm, making it nearly impossible for a non-fungible token to be considered the same as another. Tokens are digital representations of assets that have been compared to digital passports because each token carries a unique, non-transferable identity that allows it to be distinguished from the other tokens in circulation. They are alsoextendable, which means that you may combine two NFTs to create a third, one-of-a-kind NFT by breeding them together. NFTs, like Bitcoin, have ownership information that allows token holders to be easily identified and transferred between one another. In addition, NFTs enable asset owners to provide information or qualities relevant to the item. For instance, in the case of coffee beans, tokens representing the beans might be recognized as fair trade. Alternatively, artists may mark their digital artwork by including their mark in the information associated with it.

NFTs were developed because of the ERC-721 standard. ERC-721 is a smart contract standard set by some individuals liable for the ERC-20 smartcontract standard. It defines the bare minimum interface required for swapping and allocating gaming tokens, including ownership details, safety,and metadata. The ERC-1155 bar lowers the transactional and storage costs associated with non-fungible tokens while batching various NFTs into a single contract. The CryptoKitties' use of NFTs is perhaps the most well-known. CryptoKitties, which were first announced in November 2017, are digital representations of kitties that have been assigned unique identifiers on Ethereum's distributed ledger. All the kittens are different and have their ether pricing. These creatures procreate amongst themselves and generate new offspring, each of whom has unique characteristics and values compared to their parents. Following its inception, CryptoKitties quickly gained a large following, with fans spending more than $20 million in Ether (Ethereum) to purchase, feed, and otherwise care for them in their first few weeks. It is estimated that some fans spent over $100,000 on the endeavor. Though the CryptoKitties' use case may seem inconsequential, the ones that follow it have far-reaching commercial ramifications. For example, non-fungible tokens (NFTs) have been employed in private equity and real estate transactions. Incorporating numerous sorts of tokens into a single contract has many ramifications, one of which being the capacity to serve asan escrow for various forms of NFTs, ranging from art to real estate, all inside the same financial transaction.

Each NFT has a unique structure that can be used in various applications. Examples include the digital representation of tangible assets such as real estate and artwork, particularly well-suited. The fact that they are built on blockchains means that they may also be used to eliminate middlemen, link artists with audiences, or even manage user identities. NFTs can eliminate intermediaries, simplify transactions, and open up new markets.

In the present market for NFTs, collectibles such as digital artworks, sports cards, and rare items account for a significant market share. The most talked-about location is probably NBA Top Shot, where you can collect NBA NFTs in the form of digital cards. Several of these cards had fetched millions of dollars when they were auctioned. "Just setting up my Twitter," wrote Jack Dorsey in the first tweet ever written, which he sent overTwitter. The NFT of the world's first tweet has already fetched up to $2.5 million in bidding.

An NFT is just a unit of data recorded on a digital ledger known as a blockchain and maybe sold and exchanged in the cryptocurrency world. When an NFT is linked with a specific physical or digital asset, the asset may be used for a particular purpose, and the NFT can be used to grant permission to use the property for that purpose. An NFT (and the related license to use copy) can be purchased and sold in the digital marketplace. In most cases, the extralegal character of NFT trading leads to an unofficial transfer of ownership over an item that has no legal foundation for implementation and which frequently confers little more than the ability to act as a social status symbol. NFTs perform the same functions as cryptographic tokens. Non-transferable tokens (NFTs) are formed when blockchains string tracks of cryptographic hash, a collection of characters specifying a collection of data, over previous records, resulting in a chain of recognizable data blocks. Because each digital file is authenticated via a digital signature, this cryptographic transaction procedure may be used to trace who owns which NFTs. On the other hand, data linkages that refer to specifics such as where the artwork iskept may become invalidated.

Importance of NFTs

Compared to the relatively basic notion of cryptocurrencies, non-fungible tokens represent a significant advancement. Modern finance systems are contained of complex trading and financing systems for a wide range of asset kinds, spanning from property investment to loan contracts to artwork, among other things. NFTs provide a huge step forward in reconstructing this infrastructure by creating virtual representations of physical assets.

The digital representation of real assets and unique identifiers are not new concepts. Nevertheless, when these ideals are joined with the advantages of a tamper-resistant blockchain of smart contracts, they become a powerful force for positive change. The efficiency of the market is perhaps the most evident advantage of NFTs. A physical item converted into a digital asset accelerates operations and eliminates mediators. The use of non-fungible tokens (NFTs) to represent digital or physical art on a blockchain removes the need for agents and enables artists to communicate with their audiences directly. They may also help to increase the efficiency of company procedures. It will be simpler for various players in the supply chain to engage with an NFT for a wine bottle, and it will aid in tracking the bottle's origin, manufacturing, and sale throughout the whole process. One of Ernst & Young's customers has already benefited from such a solution designed by the consulting company. NFTs are also suitable for use in the context of identity management. Consider the example of real passports, which mustbe shown at every entrance and departure point. When individuals' tokens are converted into National Identification

Cards, it becomes possible to simplify the access and leave procedures for jurisdictions worldwide within each unique identifying quality. Furthermore, NFTs may be utilized for identity management in the digital environment, extending the previous use case. In addition, non-fungible tokens (NFTs) may democratize investment by fractionalizing tangible assets such as real estate. It is simpler to split a virtual real estate asset between numerous owners than to divide a physical real estate asset among many owners. This tokenization principle does not have to be limited to real estate it can be applied to other purchases. As a result, artwork does not necessarily have to be owned by a single individual. Multiple people may hold the artwork's digital version, each accountable for a different portion of the painting. Such partnerships have the potential to increase the company's value and income. The establishment of new marketplaces and types of investment represents the most intriguing prospect for non-fungible tokens. Think of a chunk of land that has been subdivided into many segments, each of which comprises a distinct set of features and various sorts of property. One of the parts maybe located near a beach, another is an entertainment venue, and another is a residential neighborhood. An NFT represents a unique chunk of land, and each piece of land is valued differently based on its unique attributes. It is possible to make real estate dealing, which is a complicated andbureaucratic endeavor, more straightforward by adding important information into each NFT.

The blockchain-based virtual reality platform Decentraland, which runs on Ethereum's network, has already implemented this notion. As non-fungible tokens (NFTs) grow more advanced and are connected to the finance system, it may become feasible to apply the same idea of tokenized parcels of land, each with various values and locations, in the real world.

Plagiarism in NFTs

There have been instances when "artists' work" has been duplicated without their consent and marketed as a non-fungible token. The designer Qing Han departed in 2020, and a scammer used her identity to sell a bunchof her paintings as non-fungible tokens (NFTs) after she was discovered to be deceased. In a similar vein, a seller portraying as Banksy sold an NFT created by the designer for $336,000 in 2021, but the seller in the given instance reimbursed the money when the matter received widespread media notice.

It is also thinkable for a scammer to mint an NFT inside an artist's wallet and then transfer it to their wallet without the artist's knowledge using a practice known as "sleepminting." It is provided an opportunity for hackers to create a bogus NFT that seemed to have come from the wallet of an American artist known as Beeple. According to the BBC, on the NFT marketplace, OpenSea, employees engaged in insider trading when they purchased NFTs before being introduced. They understood what they would be advertised on their main website before launching. NFT buying and selling is an unregulated industry with no legal repercussions for those who engage in such misconduct.

Adobe suggested the creation of a database for the cosmos, File System, as an alternate method of confirming the validity of digital works when they announced the development of NFT compatibility for the graphic editor Photoshop in their release of NFT support for Photoshop.

Owning an NFT does not automatically confer intellectual property rights on the digital asset that the token represents, as is often believed. Even though somebody might sell an NFT reflecting their work, the new buyer will not automatically obtain copyright protections when custody of the NFT is transferred. As a result, the original owner will be permitted to generate more NFTs representing the same work. An NFT is just evidence of possession that is distinct from copyright protection. Rebecca Tushnet, a law researcher, claims that "in a sense, the purchaser obtains whichever the art world believes they have received when they make the purchase. Unless the copyright to the actual work is expressly transferred, they do not in any way own the rights to it." However, customers of NFTs do not often obtain ownership of the original artwork.

Chapter 2 - History of NFT

Quantum, the first known NFT, was produced by Kevin McCoy & Anil Dash in May 2014 and consisted of a video clip generated by McCoy's wife Jennifer and other components. During a live session for Seven-on-Seven conferences at the New Museum of New York, McCoy entered the footage on the Namecoin network and sold it to Dash for $4 on the Namecoin network. As McCoy and Dash put it, the technique was referred to as"monetized graphics." A non-fungible, which was expressly tied to a one- of-a-kind piece of art (enabled by Namecoin). Compared to the multiple-unit, exchangeable "colored coins" of those other blockchains, including Counterparty, are not fungible and do not include metadata.

Three calendar months after making the Ethereum blockchain, the very first NFT venture, Etheria, was announced and exhibited at DEVCON 1, Ethereum's inaugural developer conference, in London, United Kingdom, in October 2015. After not getting sold for more than five years, most of Etheria's 457 tradable hexagonal tiles were finally snapped up on 13 March

2021, when revived interest in NFTs ignited a purchasing frenzy. For a total of $1.4 million, all tiles were sold in less than 24 hours.

The release of the ERC-721 standard initially suggested on the Ethereum GitHub in 2017 was followed by the launch of several NFT initiatives that year. The word NFT received widespread acceptance. Curio Cards, CryptoPunks (a project to trade one-of-a-kind cartoon characters, developed by the American company Larva Labs and distributed on the Ethereum blockchain), and the Decentraland platform are examples of such projects. All three initiatives were mentioned in the initial proposal, and a set of unique Pepe trading cards were included.

The popularity of CryptoKitties, a blockchain game in which participants adopt and exchange virtual kittens, sparked public interest in non-fungible tokens. Soon after its introduction, the idea went viral, generating $12.5 million and resulting in the sale of certain kittens for more than $100,000 per kitty. The popularity of CryptoKitties led to the addition of CryptoKitties to the ERC-721 standards, which was formed in January 2018 (and completed in June). It confirmed the usage of the phrase "non-fungible token" to refer to NFT.

In 2018, Decentraland, a virtual world based on blockchain that launched its token sales in August 2017, $20 million was the size of its internal market. As of September 2018, $26 million were raised in an "ico" (initial coin offering) and had a total market capitalization of $26 million.

Following the success of CryptoKitties, another comparable NFT-basedonline game, Axie Infinity, was created in March 2018 and ended up becoming the most expensive NFT collection in May 2021, after which it was discontinued.

In 2019, Nike received a patent for a system known as CryptoKicks, which would employ NFTs to check the integrity of actual shoes and provide the consumer with a virtual replica of the shoe in exchange for their payment.

During the first quarter of 2020, Dapper Labs, the company that created CryptoKitties, unveiled the preview version of NBA Top Shot, a projectthat would offer tokenized memorabilia of NBA highlights.

The project was created on top of the Flow blockchain, a younger and more powerful blockchain than the Ethereum blockchain.

Later that year, the program was made available to the public, and as of 28 February 2021, it has generated over $230 million in total revenues.

During 2020, the NFT market enjoyed fast expansion, with its total value doubling to $250 million. NFTs accounted for more than $200 million in spending during the first three months of 2021.

Following a series of high-profile transactions, interest in non-fungible tokens (NFTs) rose in the first few months of 2021. Digital art made by the artist Grimes, the NFT of a Nyan Cat meme, and NFTs designed by 3LAU to advertise his album *Ultraviolet* were among the NFTs sold in February 2021. NFT sales were made in more publicized ways in March 2021, including an NFT created to market the Kings of Leon album *When You See Yourself*, a $69.3 million sale of digital work by Mike Winkelmann titled *Everydays: the First 5000 Days*, and an NFT created by the founder of Twitter Jack Dorsey that represented his first tweet. Because of the nature of the NFT market, more investors are trading at higher volumes and rates. Experts have referred to the recent spike in NFT purchases as an economic bubble and have likened this to the Dot-com boom. By the middle of April 2021, demand looked to have significantly waned, resulting in a dramatic drop in prices; early purchasers were said to have "done extraordinarily well" by the publication

Bloomberg Businessweek. Sotheby's in London auctioned off an NFT of the source code for the World Wide Web, which was ascribed to internet creator computer scientist Professor Tim Berners- Lee in June 2021, and the piece went for US$5.4 million.

According to the auction house, Sotheby's auctioned around 101 NFTs(Bored Ape Yacht Club) worth $24.4 million in September 2021. ETH393 ($1.3 million) was paid for a complete set of Curio Cards, including the "17b" mistake on 1 October 2021, marking the first time that lives to bid at an auction was handled in Ether. A CryptoPunk, other cat-based NFTs, and a Pepenopoulos, rare Pepe, 2016, were sold for a combined total of $3.6 million at a Sotheby's auction later that month. In addition, this was the firstauction presented on Sotheby's "Metaverse," a platform devoted particularlyto NFT collectors, and it is planned to become a biennial event.

During the 27 March 2021 Saturday Night Live episode, characters explained non-fungible tokens (NFTs) to Treasury Secretary of US Janet Yellen, who Kate McKinnon portrayed.

A grown-up version of Butters Stotch in his Dr. Chaos avatar tricked people into buying NFTs in the Paramount+ TV film *South Park: Post Covid: The*

Return of Covid, which aired on Cartoon Network in 2013. Even though they are shown as a bad investment in the film, he has become so skilled at selling them that he has been sent to a mental facility.

First NFT

So, what is the root of this technological craze? NFTs and the man who designed them, Kevin McCoy, have a storied history that began on 3 May 2014. Quantum, a non-fungible currency, was established by him long before the crypto art business took off.

Quantum appears to be a pixelated design of an octagon crammed with forms that all share the same center, with more oversized shapes enclosing smaller firms and fascinating pulsating in dazzling hues, as shown on the Quantum website. It is now on the market for $7 million as part of only one "Quantum" art project (2014–2021).

McCoy is a one-of-a-kind figure in the Star Trek universe. Throughout the years, he and his girlfriend Jennifer have established themselves as the best digital painters in the industry. In McCoy's opinion, "the NFT phenomenon is deeply established in the art business." "It evolved out of a long custom of artists trying out new technology," says the author. As McCoy has done, the artist prefers to sell their work via galleries or one-on-one rather than participating in public pricing battles. The exhibit *Every Episode, Every Shot* is presently on display at the Art Museum. Artists, entrepreneurs, businesses, writers and filmmakers, social media superstars, and even everyday people may create an NFT by collaborating. There is no need for previous expertise, and anyone may mint an NFT as faras they can demonstrate that they generated or legally held the material in question. To get started using Portion, follow our step-by-step instructions on designing an NFT.

CryptoPunks & CryptoKitties are only a few cultural trends that inspired the CryptoArt genre. Due to extensive network effects and the desire to pay considerable amounts of money to acquire them, these pieces of "art"became renowned.

2012–2013

Let's start this journey including various people, artists, and organizations.A "colored coin influenced NFTs," initially launched on the Bitcoin blockchain in 2012–2013 and has since gained widespread acceptance.Colored coins are blockchain technology tokens that represent real-world assets. They may be used to prove ownership of a wide range of assets, including metals, autos, real industrial property, stocks, and bonds, among other things. The initial idea was to use the Bitcoin network to store digital artifacts such as coupons, real estate, corporate shares, and different typesof information. They were regarded as cutting-edge technology with the significant unmet possibility of future applications in several fields.

2014

A mentorship banking platform with a distributed, open-web protocol based on the Bitcoin blockchain was built in 2014 by R. Dermody and E. Wagner as part of the Bitcoin blockchain community. Counterparty created a framework for anyone to develop their transferrable currencies/coins by allowing for asset creation and decentralized exchange, which enabled them to do so. It had a plethora of excellent ideas and opportunities, particularly in meme trading without the issues associated with counterfeiting.

2015

Counterparty formed a collaboration with the Spells of Genesis creators in April 2015. Using Counterparty, the developers of the videogame Spells of Genesis were not only among the first to put in-game assets into a blockchain, but they were also among the first to make an initial coin offering (ICO). The creators of Counterparty were able to contribute to the game's development by creating their in-game currency, BitCrystals.

2017

The characters developed by J. Watkinson & M. Hall, the inventors ofLarva Labs, are one-of-a-kind. In recent years, rare Pepe's trade has gained popularity on the Ethereum platform. There'd be no two characters thatwere the same, and the total number of characters would be limited to 10,000 characters in total. The term CryptoPunks relates to a Bitcoin experiment from the 1990s, and the project may be thought of as a hybrid ofthe ERC721 and ERC20 protocols.

CryptoKitties NFTs were created with the help of the ERC721 protocol. They are a digital game based on the Ethereum network that allows players to adopt, foster, and trade virtual cats with other players across the world. They were incredibly well-known, and their appearances on major news sites such as CNBC & Fox News were well-publicized. Axiom Zen, a Vancouver-based company, created CryptoKitties, and it quickly gained popularity, garnering money from famous investors due to its fast expansion. When Axiom Zen acquired CryptoKitties, Dapper Labs wasrenamed to distinguish it from the original company.

2018–2021

NFTs progressively acquire public attention between 2018 and 2021 before exploding into widespread usage in the first half of 2021.

The allegedly secret movement that has swept the crypto realm hasgradually grown into a more widely recognized kind of art and culture.

The non-fungible tokens services business is more efficient and liquid than conventional asset-transfer strategies. Several internet platforms have sprung up, each with its features for both manufacturers and collectors. The most significant area of disruption is focused on reducing centralized fees, which can be as high as 40% for conventional art traders and auction houses. The OpenSea is the most critical market for art, music, souvenirs domain names, and trading cards globally. Mintable's platform is intended to make the minting process as easy as possible for authors, and it does so via the use of APIs. According to the section, an NFT system permits Defis,NFTs, and DAOs, with the society controlling the governing token, whichis $PRT. The purchase of "shards," which are ERC20 tokens representing a piece of a full NFT, is also likely on other platforms, such as Nintex, which allows users to buy fractions of NFTs, sometimes known as "fractions of NFTs."

Metaverse: The Future

Numerous companies are now involved in the development of virtual reality metaverses. Metaverses are virtual environments where the internetis brought to life in its simplest form. You can create your own life, interact with real individuals in an online community, design your avatar, play, work, and explore new spaces by utilizing virtual reality headsets or virtual or augmented glasses, smartphone apps, or other devices that incorporate virtual touch to create a metaverse world of your own. When it comes to metaverses, you are probably already aware of the concept if you have ever seen the *Ready Player*

One movie. At the same time, virtual worlds are being envisioned and constructed with the assistance of improved artificial intelligence, the implementation of universal standards, and the ever- increasing performance of computer processing power. You and your children will be able to visit metaverses, making today's internet appear as if it were a silent movie compared to the internet of tomorrow.

NFTs will be a critical component of metaverses, serving as the basic components for assets that may be used in any of these worlds, regardless of where they are located. As you create your virtual house, you will fill the walls with original NFT art and "prints" of replicated visual art that you have purchased from collectors to decorate it. Then you host a gathering of friends in your immersive digital home, where they can enjoy the music you've collected and admire your NFT art, which now symbolizes not just a creator's original work but also its history and the tale of how you came to be the proud owner of that art piece. Your pals come in an instant, without the use of fossil fuels or the need for an Uber. You may have been disappointed that they didn't stop all along the way to pick up chips, but they offered new digital clothing for your avatar as a housewarming present.

Metaverse will become more integrated with the actual world due to NFTs. Exact locations will have digital equivalents in virtual space, and NFT art galleries will exist in the physical world and on digital screens. Music performances will be staged in a concert hall and a virtual bar, to name a few examples. These NFTs will be sold to you as part of your virtual library of concert tickets, which will be displayed in your virtual house and include an e-signature/personalized greeting from the artist, which will be sent directly to you.

Chapter 3 - NFT and Blockchains

Blockchains

A blockchain is a decentralized software network that serves as a digital record and a platform for the safe transfer of funds without requiring a thirdparty to act as an intermediary. Like how the internet supports the digital information flow, blockchain is a distributed ledger that keeps the digital exchange of units of value in the same way that the internet promotes the movement of information. On a blockchain network, anything from currency to land titles to voting may be tokenized, recorded, and transferred, and this includes votes themselves.

The Bitcoin, a peer-to-peer electronic currency system that is safe, censorship-resistant, and decentralized, was the first embodiment of blockchain technology, appearing in 2009. Bitcoin is an open or permission-less blockchain model since it is available to anybody whowants to use it. There are several different types of blockchain technology available today. Several blockchains have been created to satisfy the demands of a small number of players, and network access is limited for these people. These are also instances of private blockchains.

Blockchain technology creates a permanent forensic record of every transaction and a single version of the truth, in addition to ensuring the safe movement of currency. This network state is completely visible and exhibited in real-time for the advantage of all players. However, irrespective of the nature of the implemented blockchain network, blockchain technology holds great promise for transforming nearly a century-old business models, laying the groundwork for higher levels of credibility in government, and opening up new avenues for economic opportunity for everyday citizens.

The unique identification and possession of an NFT may be verified via blockchain ledger technology. The NFT is often coupled with a permit to use the fundamental digital asset. In most cases, the buyer does not get ownership of the underlying digital asset. In some instances, permissionsare exclusively granted for individual, non-commercial use, and in other cases, licenses are also given for commercial use of the actual digital asset

Digital Art

Due to the blockchain's capacity to ensure the unique identifier and ownership of NFTs, digital art was one of the first applications for NFTs to emerge. As I said before, in 2021, the artist Mike Winkelmann (better known by his stage name Beeple) sold a digital artwork named *Everydays: the First 5000 Days* for US$69.3 million, the highest price ever paid for a computer artwork. It was the third-highest auction price ever achieved as a living artist, behind only pieces by Jeff Koons & David Hockney, who each earned $1 million.

Blockchain has also been used for the public registration and authentication of existent physical artworks to distinguish them from counterfeit and certify their ownership via the use of physical trackers or labels, among other applications. In March 2021, Nifty Gateway sold another Beeplework, Crossroad, a ten-second movie depicting animated people just going past a depiction of Donald Trump, and the item sold for US$6.6 million.

In the Post-War to Current auction at Christie's, Curio Cards, a digitalcollection of 30 unique cards thought to be the 1st NFT art collector's items on the Ethereum network, sold for $1.2 million, thus making the NFT most expensive art collectible ever sold. The lot also included the card "17b," which was a digital "printing error."

The EtherRocks and CryptoPunks collections, among others, are instances of generative art. A wide variety of pictures may be made by combining a selection of basic visual components in various configurations.

Blockchain Standards

Token standards were developed to accommodate a wide range of blockchain-based applications. Ethereum, with its ERC-721 average, was the first network to allow non-fungible tokens (NFTs), and it is presentlythe most extensively utilized. Because of the increasing popularity of NFTs, several other blockchains have incorporated or intend to add support for them.

Ethereum

ERC-721 was the first protocol for expressing digital assets that are non- fungible on the Ethereum blockchain, and it is the most widely used even today. Rigidity smart contract standard ERC-721 is inheritable, which means that developers may construct new ERC-721-compliant deals by importing existing ERC-721-compliant contracts from the Open Zeppelin library. When an asset has a unique identity, ERC-721 offers fundamental methods that enable the owner to be tracked down and provide permission means to transfer the item or purchase to others. The ERC-1155 standard provides "semi-fungibility," as well as a superset of the capabilities provided by the ERC-721 standard. In contrast to ERC-721 tokens, which have a unique ID representing a single asset, ERC-1155 tokens have a unique ID representing a class of support, with an extra quantity field to reflect the amount of a specific class wallet has. Transferring assets between types is possible, and the user may move any number of assets between classes at any point in time.

The present high transaction costs (also known as gas fees) associated with Ethereum have prompted the development of layer 2 solutions for the cryptocurrency, which also allow NFTs:

- A layer 2 network for Ethereum created exclusively for NFTs; Immutable X uses ZK rollups to remove gas expenses from transaction fees, allowing it to be used with other NFT protocols.

A proof-of-stake network originally referred to as the

Matic Network. Polygon is backed by major NFT markets such as OpenSea and is a fork of the Ethereum blockchain.

Different Blockchains

It is likely to buy and sell NFTs using Bitcoin Cash, which is the currency that drives the Jungle NFT exchange.

Including its March 2021 update, Cardano added native tokens that allow for the construction of NFTs without the need for smart contracts. CNFT and Theos are two of Cardano's NFT markets.

Proof of stake consensus mechanism, the Flow blockchain, enables NFTs. There are plans to transition from ETH to Flow in the coming future for CryptoKitties.

Powered by GoChain, the "eco-friendly" blockchain, the Zeromint NFT marketplace, and the VeVe app run on GoChain.

Non-fungible tokens are supported by the Solana blockchain as well. It is a proof-of-stake blockchain network that facilitates the selling ofNFT art and is known as "Tezos."

Off-Chain Storage

Due to the file's size, most NFTs incorporating digital art do not save it on the blockchain. The token operates more like a certification of ownership, along with a website address referring to the work of art in issue, implying that the work of art is still vulnerable to link rot. Because NFTs are functionally distinct from the base artworks, anybody may readily save a copy of the picture of an NFT, most often with a right-click. NFT supporters dismiss this copying of NFT artistry as a "right-clicker mindset,"with one collector equating the value of a bought NFT to that of a symbolof status "to demonstrate how they can afford to spend that much.".

The expression "right-clicker mindset" quickly gained popularity after its debut, notably among those skeptical of the NFT marketplace, who used it to demonstrate the ease with which digital art supported by NFT could be captured. Geoffrey Huntley, an Australian programmer, reinforced this critique when he constructed "The NFT Bay," a clone of The Pirate Bay. The NFT Bay marketed a torrent file containing 19 gigabytes of NFTdigital art. Huntley likened his endeavor to a Pauline Pantsdown art piece and hoped that the site would educate visitors about what NFTs are and aren't.

Use of Blockchain by NFTs

NFTs provide the capacity to assign/claim ownership of any one-of-a-kind piece of digital data that can be tracked using Ethereum's network as a public ledger, allowing anybody to participate in the digital economy. A non-fungible token (NFT) is a digital entity that may depict digital or non- digital assets.

NFTs are rapidly all-encompassing over the world of digital art and collectibles, and for a good reason. Digital artists are witnessing a transformation in their livelihood because sales are being made to a new audience. Celebrities are also hopping on board to see a unique chance to connect with their followers. Nevertheless, digital art is just one use of NFTs. Realistically, they may be used to symbolize possession of any exclusive object, such as an action for property in either the physical or digital world.

If Andy Warhol were born in the late 1990s, he would almost certainly have coined Campbell's Soup as a non-fungible token.

Concerns About the Environment

In the context of blockchain transactions, the purchase and sale of NFTs are embroiled in a debate concerning the high energy consumption and resulting greenhouse gas emissions connected with such transactions.

In particular, the proof-of-work mechanism is necessary to govern and validate the transactions. Estimating the environmental footprint of a provided NFT transaction requires making several assumptions about how that specific NFT transaction is set up on a blockchain, the economic behavior of blockchain miners (as well as the energy needed of their mining equipment), as well as the quantity of renewable energy that is being used on these networks. Other questions concern the nature of the carbon footprint estimates for NFT purchases, such as whether the estimated carbon footprint for an NFT purchase should consider some portion of the currently underway energy needs of the underlying network or only the marginal effect of that particular purchase. For this, an analog has been provided in the high carbon footprint connected with an extra passenger on a specific airline trip.

Newer NFT systems include alternative validation

methods like proof of stake, which need much less energy for a particular validation cycle than traditional protocols. More techniques to reduce power use include online transactions as part of the minting process for a non-fungible token. A couple of NFT art sites are also attempting to address these problems, with some opting to use technologies and protocols with smaller environmental footprints. Others are now offering the opportunity to purchase carbon offsets while making NFT purchases, albeit the ecological advantages have been called into doubt. NFT artists have decided not to sell part of their very own work to reduce their carbon emission commitments in certain circumstances.

Because NFTs are becoming more popular, they are also becoming the subject of heightened scrutiny, particularly regarding their carbon impact.

To be clear on a few points:

- Non-fungible tokens (NFTs) do not directly contribute to the carbon output of Ethereum.
- Ethereum's method of keeping your dollars and assets safe is now energy-intensive, but it is on the verge of becoming less so.
- Once it has been enhanced, Ethereum's carbon output will be 99.95% lower, making it more

energy-efficient than many other sectors now in use.

Blockchains Supporting NFTs

Since its introduction in the mid-2010s, non-fungible tokens (NFTs) had seen a surge in popularity, which peaked in February 2021 when Beeple's *Everydays NFT* was sold for a world-record-breaking $69.3 million.

Since then, NFTs have gained widespread acceptance and are now availablefor purchase on various online marketplaces and backed by several different blockchains.

List of the most famous blockchains compatible with NFTs other thanEthereum network:

Zilliqa

Zilliqa, which was launched in 2017, is the world's first-ever public sharding-based blockchain, according to the company. Zilliqa is meant to bemore resilient regarding scalability, which means that network expansion does not influence transaction performance. Early blockchains, such asBitcoin and Ethereum, were infamous for the slowness they processed transactions.

Flow

Proof-of-stake blockchain, Flow, is primarily built to serve NFTs and other consumer-oriented applications. Dapper Labs, the creators of CryptoKitties,among the first games based on NFTs, developed Flow in response to the Ethereum network being clogged due to CryptoKitties transactions in 2017

Tezos

Tezos is a proof-of-stake blockchain introduced in 2018 and is open-source software. Tezos fosters involvement and cooperation with the users for continuous improvement and long-term upgradeability due to its open-source nature. Compared to Ethereum, Tezos stresses many advantages, the most notable of which is its eco-friendliness, since it requires 2 million times less power and much less than 1 XTZ to mint 1 NFT than Ethereum.

Solana

According to its developers, Solana is a proof-of-stake blockchain that promises to be the quickest in the world. Unquestionably, one of the most attractive characteristics of Solana is its capacity to scale, which ensuresthat the network will always be speedy while also guaranteeing that on the web, no transaction will ever surpass $0.01

Cardano

Cardano is a blockchain that operates on the proof-of-stake principle and is open-source. It has a formidable team behind it, including the Ethereum co-founder, and it emphasizes the necessity of regulatory compliance andscalability in its development. It also promises to become the most ecologically friendly blockchain technology available.

Chapter 4 - What Are Some of the Most Popular NFTs?

Non-fungible tokens (NFTs) have been widely used in digital money because they may be used to convey information uniquely while maintaining ownership of the data.

In turn, they've progressed beyond what we might expect from a digital token as a simple measure of wealth, becoming a collectible item with an endless variety of heads, as B. Allen explains: "Folks adore to collect things, whether it's sporting events cards, bottle caps, or matchbooks; NFTs satisfy this desire without taking up physical space." Aside from that, they also offer a substantial potential upside, meaning that a $100 purchasemight potentially turn into $1,000 there in the future, comparable to investing in the secondary art market. Given the fact that NFTs are acutting-edge innovation, they appeal to people who are willing to break the mound and attempt something new and exciting." The well-known natureof NFTs has been employed to create single and engaging viewers' experiences in other media. Robert Alice's NFT, which was produced in collaboration with Alethia.AI, was recently sold off by Sotheby's and the New York Foundation for the Arts. FAMILY has unveiled its BoringStone Genesis Collection, part of a wider NFT project that includes members of the greater NFT community as participants.

According to L. Rensing, founder and chairman of enterprise bitcoin solutions provider Protokol, the popularity of NFTs in the sports and entertainment space provided an opportunity to participate with fans at a time when traditional avenues for doing so were closed due to the pandemic: "The prominence of NFTs in the sports and entertainment room offered a chance to engage in fanning base at a time when conventional lines of inquiry for doing so were shuttered due to the pandemic."

So, from the Kings of Leon releasing their current album as an NFT to the success of NBA Greatest Shots and WePlay Esports' NFTs, it shows many athletes, video game teams, performers, and musicians jump into the ring to make their mark. If done correctly, NFTs have the potential to generate significant long-term growth while also increasing fan engagement.

Issuers may be able to accomplish this by trying to make NFTs more than just digital collectibles, rather than simply offering them as individualized rewards for fan loyalty and participation.

The Emergence of NFTs

At the Token 2049 festival *NFTs: From Zero to One*, the visual artist spoke about her collaboration with S. Aoki and cited meme/gif society and political mainstream press as the quickest propulsion systems for the rising global popularity of NFTs. She added: "I'm excited about this collaboration. I believe that memes and gifs are a part of this process because they are the most efficient means of spreading information. When users consider a marketing strategy, each time a few of these memes/gifs is effective, you will see it and have the opportunity to use it."

To summarize, "creating an effective meme requires anticipating the NFTs hit rate among normal people and relying on a small amount of luck or chance, which no one can comprehend; this is the most difficult aspect of the process. So sometimes a meme starts, but other times it's completely random, and this is why I believe it's highly beneficial to analyze what others do and watch, and it may be the most effective tool for people to publicize; the foundation of an electronic token market, to name a few examples" according to the author.

Among the most appealing characteristics of NFTs is their ability to keep the owner's true identity, which distinguishes them as a contemporary step forward in the evolution of the art world. According to Bradley Miles, CEOas well as co-founder of Roll's, "NFTs is an early demonstration of howboth the artist and the users may economically hold the content. They are reversing the traditional ownership model. Ownership of the content or itemremains solely with the creator, and the platform is only a method for the user to show, trade, or otherwise make use of what they have created. Even though NFTs are a unique paradigm, they are fundamentally aligned with artists in that they provide them with more economic control over thecontent they create on the internet."

According to H. Sheikh, "one of the reasons why NFTs make owningdigital art so enticing is the element of genuineness it provides. It has fundamentally altered the way we defend our digital intellectual property rights." Like V. Pestritto, Partner Programs Manager of Agoric, notes, "NFTs are a coupled business reason to a marketplace that loves the idea of irreparable ownership. In the past few weeks, I've met small business owners who are also art collectors. They're purchasing non-traditional works of art because of the evident relevance and culture associated with owning art. People who work in the crypto industry as artists and depend on their day jobs to finance their passion have identified a clear opportunity to reach out now to crypto enthusiasts who recognize the unique feature of the NFT/artwork developed."

Value of NFTs

Even though NFTs allow people to represent, store, and trade their resources, do they have any lengthy value? NFTs are distinguished from other collectibles by the possibility of an unexpected financial failure. The value of an NFT is determined by the public's perception of its worth, including its exclusivity and rarity. D. Weragoda, MBANC's CTO (Chief Technology Officer), explains that "most individuals don't comprehend the key technical NFTs, or even what NFTs is, and you'll have to comprehend what you're entering into before you start spending money into hyped-up illusions."

However, this type of conduct has led many individuals to lose money in other financial markets, such as Bitcoin. "Be careful when tying non- fungible tokens to anything that provides true use, since what exactly are you buying in? The fact that it's a new child on the block means that there's a massive industry for buzzwordy technology. Since we all understand, the bitcoin has a very short attention span," H. Sheikh writes on evaluating the actual price of an NFT if there are no tangible criteria to justify the pricing of the NFT. Given the rapid shift in public opinion, if the thing is to be used as a measure of wealth, it is necessary to identify the criteria by which the item's worth will be assessed in the future.

The NFT has "a sense of worth," but it is impossible to attribute a genuine value to it without first understanding where the true value derives from. Consequently, the current pattern is no longer viable in the long run. If non-fungible tokens (NFTs) are used to prove ownership of property riches, like real estate, they will become a feasible trend. The community's evaluation of whether or not a specific NFTs' value will continue to climb decides whether or not that asset is regarded as a desirable item in the first place. There has to be a more quantitative technique for estimating a non-fungible token's future value.

Perspectives for the Future

It is estimated that the increase around the world in NFTs more than doubled in the short time between July and August 2021, surpassing 1.3 million unique buyers and sellers, according to Statista figures. Recently released data from NonFungible.com revealed that NFT sales reached between $10 million and $20 million per week, with weekly transaction volume increasing by approximately 300% during various times of the year. Is the increasing popularity of NFTs here to remain, or will they be a relicof the past shortly?

According to Brittany Allen, who is concerned about their long-term survival, considering that NFTs are still in their infancy, it's hard to predict what form they will take in the future. "After subsequent buys of NFTs start to earn value—or at the very least sustain interest—I believe they will become a permanent fixture in the financial landscape. There would inevitably be failures along the way," she goes on to say.

"In the case of early adult literature, for example, once literature Twitterwas revealed to be infringing on the copyrights of children, this NFT attempt failed, highlighting the necessity of investors making educated judgments at such a young point in the industry's lifespan. Numerical fractions are all here to live, and their use will continue to expand inside the art world, into artist collaborations and assistance for secondary market transactions, and outside the art world, into other unique scenarios for businesses," Vanessa Pestritto expresses herself. NFTs for small businesses can generate a more trustworthy link between transacting parties in various situations, including commercial invoices, theater tickets, and printing more money in the case of projects and collaboration. However, James K. Cropcho advises against adopting NFTs to earn quick money in the near term: "NFTs is both a trend and something that will be there for a long time." Nevertheless, because NFTs are a novel and, as a result, "bright and new" item, many individuals who would not normally collect have experimented in the industry; however, many of them are likely searching for quick cash to supplement their income. However, even though several periodicals and news shows have covered the matter, usually with a disdainful air of goofiness rather than an attempt at serious explication, NFTs are not widely accepted. Based on pure speculation, I assume that the global market for NFTs is less than the global market for jellyfish.

Popular NFTs

Over the past several generations, non-fungible tokens have become a popular financial notion. While many uses for these bitcoin assets are still in the early stages of development, art investment has surfaced as an initial NFT success story. Traditional art investment was mostly reserved for the rich, but non-fungible tokens (NFTs) have opened up art purchasing and selling to the public. There are a few and far between ideas you need to be familiar with before getting started, one of which is what the greatest NFT art presently looks like. They are excellent investments in which to gain money.

CryptoPunks

CryptoPunks were 10,000 one-of-a-kind pixelated pictures of a varied range of characters created by Larva Labs. The blockchain-based art effort Larva Labs was among the earliest NFT art successes, and it was based on Ethereum's blockchain. The CryptoPunk program, first made available for free in 2017, has since gained widespread attention on social media. Paintings resold for millions of dollars have been a common occurrence.

Beeple

Mike Winkelman, better known by his alias Beeple, is a very well New Frontiers of Technology artist. In actuality, Christie's sold it off NFT-based artwork *Everydays: The First 5,000 Days* of even more than $69 million in March 2021, assisting in bringing NFT artwork into the public's attentionfor the first time. Beeple has been publishing a digital photo every day for more than 13 years, so his new work is in high demand, commanding high prices.

Bored Ape Yacht Club

It is a collection of 10,000 ape pictures from comic books that the author created. Each piece functions as a collector's item and an online membership card, granting owners access to a virtual environment designed specifically for the ape avatar. Even if the NFTs are sold out, you may still purchase them from owner-occupiers via an NFT market such as OpenSea. Huge sums of cash have previously been spent on the company's most expensive BAYCs.

Axie Infinity

Axie Infinite would be a bitcoin computer game created on the Ethereum platform and is available for download. Player's usage of Axies, fanciful animals that can be taught, bred to produce more Axies, and acquired and sold using Axie Shards, is utilized to participate in various tournaments. Hundreds and thousands of users log on to play Axie Infinity every day, andthe most precious Axies may fetch thousands of dollars on the Ethereum cryptocurrency market. Pokémon-themed non-fungible token (NFT) videogame established on the Ethereum blockchain, Axie Infinity, is inspired by the mythology of the Pokémon franchise. Millions of Axies, attractive fantasy creatures can be raised, battled, and skilled as digital pets, which users may acquire, nurture, battle, and skill. Its primary idea is "play-to-earn," according to which gamers are compensated for the time andeffort they put in. These advantages are provided in the form of an SLPcoin, which you may acquire via normal gaming activities. Axie Infinity is possibly the best cryptocurrency concept ever conceived. Everything isbuilt and refined from the user experience to tokenomics with meticulous attention to detail. It is presently the costliest NFT series, with a market value of $42 million in 2021, with sales of a further $1 billion per year expected for the following year. It works with various platforms, including Windows, Macintosh, iOS, and Android. To do this, they want to create a virtual market where people can own and manage enterprises while also saving, trading, and consuming payments without traveling to a bank.

Gods Unchained

Developers may access decks and participate in a game against one another in this free and easy-to-play trading card game. Gods Unchained seems tobe a trading card game in the manner of Magic the Gathering. Because ofits great in-game components and creative animations, every statement on the presidential website has increased to $1.3 million in less than a month, a significant increase from the previous month. Because the cards are verifiable property in Ethereum, all parties have ownership of their assets. Griffith, The Chosen, is an NFT card that appears in an instance. Gods Unchained seems to be the leading supplier of card game games, thanks to a freshly launched marketplace and a plethora of exchange options that are more extensive than ever.

CryptoKitties

CryptoKitties was the first game to be established on the Ethereum network, and it remains to this day. Player's purchase, sell and breed kittens to develop desired traits represented by ERC-721 coins that are inseparable and one-of-a-kind in the game. On big NFT exchanges like opensea.io, CryptoKitties may be traded for a profit. Dapper Labs developed the game published in November 2017 on the Ethereum blockchain. Believe it or not, acquiring and caring for digital cats seems interesting to engage in. The popularity of the game, for example, resulted in congestion and the creation of national heads on the Ethereum network in 2017. It is possible to get a CryptoKitty by buying one off the market. Pairing allows individuals to get access to otherwise unavailable skills. In addition, you may win incentives by building a collection of cat figurines. Once you've amassed a large enough supply of cats, you may transfer them to the KittyVerse, where they can engage in catfights. You will also be able to team up with a group to answer puzzles if you so want.

Illuvium

It is a user-friendly role-playing adventure game with a play-to-earn design that enables players to win in-game rewards as they play. You benefit from gas charges, peer-to-peer inventing, and fast operations, all while preserving safe control over your cash and cryptocurrency. Classic role-playing game elements are combined with combat strategies established by the Autobattler genre to provide a unique gaming experience. The Illuvium video game will be made available to the public in 2022.

The Sandbox

It is a virtual metaverse in which you may own property, participate in games, and even develop your own game from scratch. Govern the huge virtual world as a collector, creator, or game judge, or simply as a player that rambles about the metaverse, moving from one game to another, if you so want. Sandbox is a virtual world established on the Ethereum platform with its currency dubbed Sand. A blockchain editor has been developed, which may be used to construct pieces and simulations for bitcoin's future edition. One of the finest games to be played if you own these digital land and real estate while also having a large presence in the metaverse is *The Elder Scrolls: Legends of the Fallen.*

Buzzwords for NFTs

At their most basic level, most NFTs are Ethereum blockchain components. Ethereum is a cryptocurrency, like Bitcoin and Dogecoin. These NFTs, on the other hand, are enabled by blockchain, which holds additional information that allows them to operate only on an ETH token. It's worth noting that various blockchains may use NFTs in multiple ways. Although NFTs may be digitized (sketches, music, or even your mind being transported and transformed into an AI), the present buzz is on using technology to market digital art. As a result, I've put up a dictionary of NFT words.

PFP

"Profile picture" is abbreviated as PFP. PFP is responsible for the CryptoPunks, Meebits, beautiful kittens, and other avatars designs we use like Twitter and Discord profile photos.

DYOR

"DYOR" is an abbreviation that translates for "Do Your

Own Research." This remark is commonly used when avoiding responsibility for the issue of whether an NFT is good or harmful for you.

HODL

It is a wrong spelling of "hold" that refers to acquiring goods practices in the world of cryptocurrency and NFTs.

In a panic, sell

In contrast to holding, anxious buyers get agitated when prices fall and rush to sell whatever they've bought. A minimal cost on NFT marketplaces, the least available list price is for the whole collection rather than a piece of the series.

Metaverse

Customers may interact with a device environment and other users via the metaverse, a virtualization technique. In essence, this is the web of tomorrow.

Purchase the Dip

When a cryptocurrency's price decreases, purchase it to benefit when the price climbs again.

Derivatives

Adapted from the original projects made famous by various "alternative" punks. They have little resemblance to the initial efforts. Art that is made on the spur of the moment. Algorithmically made art, preferably in real-time asit is coined.

FOMO

FOMO (Fear Of Missing Out) is the fear of losing out on something significant. Buying an NFT ensures that you don't miss out on another big thing.

Ethereum

Ethereum is a decentralized, open-source blockchain that enables users to build smart contracts. Ethereum is perhaps the most popular blockchain, especially among non-fungible tokens (NFTs). Ethereum is an excellent place to begin learning about this intriguing topic. They manage a large number of games. You'll discover something that interests you. Ethereum has blazed the way both with the NFT economy and the game CryptoKitties. You'll find a weblog and NFT activity monitoring data on this site. The cryptocurrency Ether (ETH) seems to be a digital asset.

The Ethereum cable network's initial cryptocurrency, Ether (ETH), is the second most popular digital token after Bitcoin (BTC). There are two sorts of ERCs: ERC-1155 and ERC-721.

Inside a single ERC-721 contract, only one token may be generated. Insidea single ERC-1155 contract, you may create many tickets.

Free for Gas

You must pay a fee to use the blockchain network. Two examples are giving funds from your account, interacting with a dap, trading tokens, or buying a collection. It's possible to think of it as a monthly cost. This price will vary based on how congested the network is because the mining in charge of completing your transactions is more likely to prioritize transactions with higher fees. The price rises as a result of congestion. Your pricing is decided by the quantity of gas needed for your payment on a technical level. Gas is the fee miners pay to generate extra data on a blockchain.

Metadata

Metadata is a set of data that uniquely defines your virtual model. The author, file size, time the site was produced, and keywords that describe the content may all be included in the metadata of an article. Metadata for just a sound file consists of the original artist, the album, and the year the music was released.

MetaMask

MetaMask is perhaps the most widely used non-custodial bank, which means you have complete control over your cash at all times. Unlike the other crypto wallets, MetaMask is built with privacy in mind. It enables you to acquire, keep, and trade tokens without having to worry about dApps or markets accessing more data than you've permitted them to. If you're using Defi applications or browsing Web 3.0 sites, MetaMask keeps you in absolute control of personal assets and data.

DAO

Decentralized Autonomous Organizations or DAOs are member-owned communities with no centralized leadership. Its goal is to empower an NFT marketplace's society and give governance via voting rights for platform improvements and moderation.

CryptoKitties

When the ICO raced and this game crowded the network, CryptoKitties remembered the horror and the delight. Everyone selected to possess an alpha cat rallying call or a rare one to make money. Assumption andmaterialism drove individuals to purchase such assets. The goal was to make money. There's nothing wrong with it. CryptoKitties came up with a great use case. CryptoKitties' creation of gaming with such a cryptocurrency overlay will go down in history. NFT will add anotherdimension to how you spend your time playing those games. You'll now devise a financial motivation, and your work will gain worth as you acquirehelpful cards and stuff over time. Perhaps, individuals will earn a full-time income from the NFT economy in the not-too-distant future. It may be closer than we believe! The hitch with non-fungible tokens is that they are about to strike the betting industry like a storm. Consider getting money every week from NTF by selling, accumulating, or trading value. In the crypto world, this is another amazing aspect of the blockchain.

Chapter 5 - How Does NFT Work?

You've undoubtedly heard of words like Bitcoin, blockchain, and, more recently, NFTs if you've been following the tech headlines lately. Artists & collectors alike have been drawn to stories of mega-dollar auctions for digital assets. But what exactly are NFTs? Also, how do they function? We'll look at the fundamentals of non-fungible tokens, cryptocurrency technology that underpins them, and how they're used in daily life. We'll also go over certain skills and expertise you'll need to join them.

The term "non-fungible token" refers to a not-fungible token. That probably doesn't imply anything at this point; the word "fungible" isn't used all that much. It does, however, imply that anything is replaceable.

Money, for example, is just a fungible asset in economics, and it is divided into units that can be readily swapped without gaining or losing value. Gold, cryptocurrencies, and stocks are all examples of fungible assets.

As we learned in the cryptocurrency open step, a fungible asset can be divided up in various ways and infinite quantities. They may be used for multiple purposes, including payments and storing value.

The non-fungible asset, on either hand, is a one-of-a-kind item, such as a painting, a home, or a trading card. Even though an artwork may be replicated or filmed, the source is the original, and reproductions are not valuable.

NFTs are electronic information units that are stored on the blockchain. Each non-fungible token acts as an authentication certificate, proving that a digital item is unique and not interchangeable. Because of the cryptographicconcepts that make blockchain unique, an NFT is never modified, amended,or stolen.

Blockchain

We've written a comprehensive guide on blockchain, cryptocurrencies, and bitcoin. We said in that piece that a blockchain is a database, a compilation of electronically recorded information or data. Unlike a traditional database, a blockchain comprises corresponding data "blocks." This blockchain chain forms a shared information ledger (data collection) that records the chain's activities and information.

Each blockchain database is kept on hundreds of separate serversworldwide. It implies that everybody on the network may see (and confirm)everyone else's entries. It's practically hard to falsify or meddle with data inside a block using this peer-to-peer & distributed ledger technology. So, according to IBM, blockchain is a distributed, irreversible (permanent and unalterable) database that makes recording transactions and monitoring assets easier. When we conceive NFTs, we think of them as being producedon a blockchain, never being transferred to another blockchain environment. It will live on the blockchain and serve as proof of the validity of the item you bought.

Digital Asset

Simply said, a digital asset is everything that exists in digital form andcould be used (a right to duplicate, copy, modify, reproduce, and otherwise use). Documents, audio or video information, photographs, and other related digital data, for example, are all termed digital assets.

Why Are NFTs Worthy?

As we've previously discussed, a non-fungible item is a license of possession for a digital asset. The value is obtained from the property's collectability and potential future selling value, and NFTs may be bought and sold.

Using art as an illustration of the gains of NFTs is a further superb example.

NFT Auctions Standards

The art of the NFT was not the only item that sold. Recently, there have been some large sales in NFTs, expressing concern that the economy has been in a bubble. The following are some instances of NFT sales:

- It is the first Tweet. Twitter's creator, Jack Dorsey, sold his NFT during his first Tweet worth $2.9 million.
- The "Nyan Cat" animated GIF. The NFT again for bright GIF was marketed for 300 Ethereum, worth almost $561,000 just at the time.
- *Charlie Bit Me* video. A video of a baby eating his brother's fingers was seen over 800 million hours on YouTube. The NFT of the video was sold for around £500,000.

What Can You Do with Non-Fungible Tokens?

Many people wonder whether there are any applications for NFTs. Even though the notion is still in its infancy, numerous possible applications have already developed. Below, we've selected a handful of the more notable ones:

Ticket

Event tickets are one of the applications of NFTs that we described in our first step. The argument is if tickets are produced that use a non-fungible token, there will be a record of that trade if the key is exchanged.

Therefore, there is no possibility of scalping, stealing, or attempting to use counterfeit tickets. Hence, the token on the blockchain linked with that ticket cannot be replaced.

Fashion

NFTs have the potential to solve several important difficulties in the fashion industry. To begin with, maintaining a permanent copy of authenticity aids in the detection of counterfeit items. An NFT might be connected to a luxury object to prove its authenticity. Likewise, a non-fungible token might provide important information about an item's origins, such as the components used, where they came from, and how far it has traveled. It might help individuals make more ethical judgments as topics like design and conservation are more prominent.

Collectables

We've previously touched on this subject. Collecting souvenirs, trinkets,and other such stuff has long been a popular pastime. NFTs act as electronicsignatures or seals of approval, confirming authenticity.

Gaming

We looked at the massive market value associated with gaming in our pieceon the video game business. NFTs allow players to possess one-of-a-type in-game objects, and such tokens may fuel in-game ecosystems, whether forenjoyment, authenticity, or competitive nature.

Working

Paintings, as well as other traditional pieces of art, are prized for their uniqueness. On either hand, digital files may be easily or endlessly replicated. Graphics may be "tokenized" using NFTs to generate a digital proof of purchase that can be purchased and sold. Will physical trading cards be phased out in favor of digital-only trade cards? A track of who owns what, like crypto-currency, is kept on a public ledger blockchain network. So, because multiple computers keep ledgers all around the globe, the data cannot be fabricated. NFTs may also include smart contracts that, for example, offer the artist a percentage of any future token sales. NFTs differ from ERC-20 tokens like DAI & LINK in that every ticket is one-of-a-kind and cannot be split. NFTs allow for the assignment or claim of possession of any individual data subject's data, which let be trailed using Ethereum's network as a shared ledger. As a portrayal of digital, non-digital properties, an NFT is created from digital items. An NFT possibly will, for standard, signify:

- Art in the Digital Age
- GIFs
- Collectibles
- Music
- Videos
- An item from the real world: Deeds to a vehicle
- Tickets to a live event in the real world
- Invoices that have been tokenized
- Documents of legal significance Signatures

There is a surplus of new options to explore!

At any moment, an NFT can have one owner. The unique information that no other tokens can reproduce is used to maintain ownership. Smart contracts which assign proprietorship & govern the NFTs are utilized to produce them. When someone generates or mints an NFT, they executecode from clever agreements that follow various standards, including ERC- 721. This data is stored on the blockchain, where the NFTs are handled. From a high level, the minting process includes the subsequent steps:

- Add together a different tower block to the matchKnowledge verification
- Containing files against the blockchain NFTs have a few exceptional characteristics:
- Each token has a unique identification tied to a single Ethereumaddress.
- They are not replaceable 1:1 with other tokens. 1 ETH, for example, isidentical to another ETH, and with NFTs, this isn't the case.
- Each coin has a unique owner whose identity can be readily verified. They are based on Ethereum and may be purchased and traded onevery Ethereum-based NFT exchange.

To put it a different way, if you acquire an NFT: It's simple to show that youown it. Demonstrating that you hold an NFT is comparable to showing that you also have ETH within your account.

Let's imagine you buy an NFT and have possession of the one-of-a-kind token transmitted to your wallet through your public address.

- The token verifies that your digital file copy is the original.
- Your private key serves as verification that you hold the original.

The originator's public key is inextricably linked to the token'shistory. The creator's access policy may be used to prove that a certain person generated the ticket you own, increasing its market worth (vs. a counterfeit).

Signing messages to confirm you possess the private key underlying the address is another technique to prove you still own NFT.

It cannot be manipulated in any manner.

You may resell it, and in certain situations, resale royalties will bepaid to the original inventor.

Alternatively, you may keep it indefinitely, safe in the knowledgethat your Ethereum wallet will protect your investment.

Also, if you make an NFT:

- You may establish that you are the creator.You determine the scarcity.
- Every time it is sold, you may receive royalties.

You may sell this on any NFT or peer-to-peer exchange. You're notattached to anyone's program, and you don't require anybody to act as an intermediary.

Scarcity

The developer of an NFT is in charge of determining the asset's scarcity. Consider purchasing a ticket to something like a sports event. The designer of an NFT may pick how many copies there are, much as an event organizercan choose how many tickets to sell. 5000 general admission tickets, for example, are sometimes exact reproductions. For example, a ticket withonly an allocated seat may be issued in multiples that are extremely similar yet somewhat different. In another scenario, the designer could seek to construct a one-of-a-kind NFT as a unique collectible.

Each NFT might still have a distinct character (like a barcode system on a typical "ticket") and only one owner in these scenarios. The NFTs intended scarcity is important, and it is up to the designer to decide. A creator might intend to create each NFT fully unique to promote absence, or they may have good cause to generate thousands of copies. Keep in thinking that all this knowledge is available to the public.

Royalties

When certain NFTs are sold, royalties are automatically sent to the creators. It is a new notion, yet it's already among the most powerful. Every time an NFT is sold, the rightful owners of Euler Beats Founders get an 8% royalty. And certain sites, like Foundation and Zora, encourage their artists to earn royalties. It is automated, so authors can sit back to collect royalties as the work is passed across from one individual to the next. Currently, calculating royalties is exceedingly laborious and inaccurate, which means many artists are underpaid. You'll rarely miss out on a royalty if your NFT is configured with one.

Increasing Creators' Earnings

The most widespread use of NFTs currently is in digital material. Since the industry is in a country of confusion today, Boards are sapping content producers' income & earning potential. An illustrator who works on a socialtelevision site makes proceeds for the podium, advertising adverts to the performer's followers. In conversation, they get publicity, but coverage doesnot pay the bills.

NFTs firewood a new innovative financial system in which creators retain control of their work rather than distribute it to the platforms that promote it. Ownership is ingrained in the substance. Whenever they sell their work, the money goes straight to them. The original author may be entitled to royalties if the new owner sells the NFT. The creator's location is part of a token's information, which can't be changed. Therefore, this is assuredevery time it's sold.

Increasing Gameplay Opportunities

NFTs have piqued the curiosity of game developers. NFTs could be appliedto monitor who owns what it is in, drive in-game economics, and provide a range of additional benefits to players.

Many regular games allow you to buy items to use in your game. However, if the weapon was an NFT, you may be able to recoup your commitment by purchasing it after the game. You may even make money if that item becomes more popular. Game designers may be royalty paid if an order is placed on the free market, consequently of their work on the NFT. Accordingly, a more mutually beneficial business model arises, in which the tertiary NFT market benefits both players and creators. It also indicates that even when the game's makers cease supporting it, the content you've amassed is yours to keep. In the end, the in-game objects you grind for may outlast the game itself, and your things will still be under your control, even if a sport is no longer supported. As a result, in-game artifacts become digital memorabilia with a value outside the game. Decentraland, a virtual world game, allows you to purchase NFTs that represent virtual land tracts as you want.

Working of Minting NFT

A few things must happen while minting an NFT:

It proves that the proposed is a blockchain asset.

The amount of the owner's account must be changed to accommodate that asset, allowing it to be exchanged or "owned" in a verifiable manner.

The transactions, as mentioned earlier, must be added to brick &"immortalized" just on-chain.

Everybody in the network must agree that the block is "correct." Because of system decides to know your

NFT originates and belongs to you, there is no need for intermediaries. It's also on the blockchain so that anybody can check it. One of the methods Ethereum assists NFT developers in maximizing their revenue is via this mechanism.

Miners oversee all these responsibilities. They also inform the entire network about their NFT and who owns it. It implies mining must be sufficiently tough; otherwise, anybody might claim possession of the NFT you just coined and transfer ownership unlawfully. There are several incentives put in place to ensure that miners operate honestly.

CPSIA information can be obtained
at www.ICGtesting.com
Printed in the USA
BVHW011933240722
642899BV00002B/6

9 781803 039411